This book is dedicated to my parents, my brothers, my sisters, my wife, and my children. Although small, it is a testament to the efforts and sacrifices that my parents made so that others could live their dreams. Thank you for creating this story that I now share with the world.

JOSE:
To my father, Jose (Chepe), who loved work and loved the land.

Lil' LIBROS
www.LilLibros.com

Mi papá es un agrícola • My Father, the Farmworker
Published by Little Libros, LLC

Text © 2023 J. Roman Pérez Varela
Art © 2023 Jose B. Ramirez
Designed by Haydeé Yañez

Library of Congress Control Number 2022944377

Printed in China
Second Edition – 2023   JHP 08/23
27 26 25 24 23   2 3 4 5
ISBN 978-1-948066-75-4

Mi papá es un agrícola

My Father, the Farmworker

Story by
J. Roman Pérez Varela

Art by
Jose Ramirez

Every morning, my father waves goodbye to the Moon and greets the Sun.

Cada mañana, mi padre se despide de la Luna y saluda al Sol.

He helps my mother prepare lunch while he enjoys a cup of coffee. The sweet aroma of fresh tortillas wafts through the house.

Ayuda a mi madre a preparar la comida mientras él disfruta de una taza de café. El dulce aroma de las tortillas frescas recorre la casa.

"I'm on my way to wake up the land," he always says.

"Voy de camino a despertar a la tierra", dice siempre.

He walks, leaving thousands of steps over Mother Earth.

Camina, dejando miles de pasos sobre la Madre Tierra.

With his hands and back, my father harvests nature's gifts: fruits and vegetables that will arrive to tables far and wide.

Con sus manos y espalda, mi padre cosecha los abundantes regalos de la naturaleza: frutas y verduras que llegarán a las mesas de todo el mundo.

Under the rain, his sweat washes away.

Bajo la lluvia, su sudor se desvanece.

Under the sun, his sweat evaporates and his skin becomes coppery.

Bajo el sol, su sudor se evapora y su piel se vuelve cobriza.

Under the cold night sky, his hands go numb as a faint cloud forms with each breath. His clothes weigh heavily like a burden he must carry.

Bajo el manto del frío, sus manos se entumecen mientras una débil nube se forma bajo cada respiro. Su ropa pesa como una carga que debe llevar.

My father's hands are cracked,
caked with mud.

Las manos de mi padre están agrietadas, cubiertas de barro.

His paisano's eyes become covered with salt and dirt. My father offers his bandana, and they both continue until the night casts stars.

Los ojos de su paisano se cubren de sal y tierra. Mi padre le ofrece su pañuelo, y ambos continúan hasta que la noche arroja estrellas.

The Moon follows him home.

La Luna lo sigue a casa.

He won't admit to it, but I can see defeat in his eyes.
I can also see hope. He dreams of what tomorrow may
bring: a future.

No lo admite, pero puedo ver la derrota en sus ojos.
También veo esperanza. Sueña con lo que puede traer el
mañana: un futuro.

He is my father, and I am proud to say he is a farmworker.

Es mi padre, y estoy orgulloso de decir que es
un trabajador agrícola.

J. Roman Pérez Varela

My father, Antonio, arrived to this country in the 1950s through the Bracero Program, a program of opportunity. His initial goal was to not live the American Dream; rather, his vision was to return to Mexico and live his dream life back home. In time, he decided to bring my mother and siblings to the USA. This book is a tribute to them and the daily ritual of hard labor they endured to allow me to share this story with you. As a child growing up in the streets of Salinas, seeing so many campesinos became a normal vision. Though my father and mother never lived their Mexican Dream, they allowed me to live my own dream here on this soil. That was the inheritance they gifted me. I'd like to return the favor: *Mi papá es un agrícola* is finally my gift to them.

Jose Ramirez

Illustrating *Mi papá es un agrícola / My Father, the Farmworker* helped me connect with my childhood memories of growing up in El Sereno, Los Angeles. My father was a carpet layer and worked all the seasons too. It was very hard work, but he was good at it. After work, he would then come home and garden. That is how I learned to garden. I hope to inspire a love of plants and food, respect, and admiration for the workers who bring us the food we eat. The paintings in this book are inspired by and dedicated to the agrícolas who work the fields, every season, from sunrise to sunset. Respect to all workers, everywhere!